Auschwitz Report

Auschwitz Report

PRIMO LEVI

with

LEONARDO DE BENEDETTI

Translated by Judith Woolf
Edited by Robert S. C. Gordon

VERSO

London • New York

First published as 'Rapporto sull'organizzazione igienico-sanitaria del campo
di concentramento per ebrei di Monowitz (Auschwitz – Alta Silesia)'
by *Minerva Medica* 1946
© Giulio Einaudi Editore
This edition published by Verso 2006
© Translation Judith Woolf 2006
© Introduction Robert S. C. Gordon 2006
All rights reserved

1 3 5 7 9 10 8 6 4 2

Verso
UK: 6 Meard Street, London W1F 0EG
USA: 180 Varick Street, New York, NY 10014-4606
www.versobooks.com

Verso is the imprint of New Left Books

ISBN-13: 978-84467-092-5
ISBN-10: 1-84467-092-9

British Library Cataloguing in Publication Data
A catalogue record for this book is available from the British Library

Library of Congress Cataloging-in-Publication Data
A catalog record for this book is available from the Library of Congress

Typeset in Perpetua by Hewer Text UK Ltd
Printed and bound in Germany by GGP Media GmbH

CONTENTS

CONTENTS

Introduction

Two Survivors

On 27 January 1945, the Soviet Red Army liberated what was left of the network of concentration, labour and extermination camps near Auschwitz (Oświęcim) in southern Poland. The first part of the camp they stumbled upon was Buna-Monowitz (Monowice), or Auschwitz III, a satellite of the central Auschwitz-Birkenau complex which was run by the Nazis in collaboration with the industrial-chemical corporation IG Farben. Until days earlier, 12,000 enslaved labourers, mostly Jews, had been kept there in appalling conditions. Amongst the several hundred sick and dying left behind by the retreating Nazis were two Italian Jews, both from Turin: 46-year-old doctor Leonardo De Benedetti and 25-year-old chemistry graduate Primo Levi.

De Benedetti and Levi had arrived in Auschwitz on the same train convoy, probably in the same cattle-truck, almost exactly eleven months earlier, on 26 February 1944, after a horrific four-day journey from a detention camp at Fossoli in central Italy. They had first met at Fossoli in early 1944, after being arrested in December 1943 in different parts of the mountains north and west of Turin. De Benedetti was picked up by Italian militia near Como with his wife Jolanda, after they had failed to find sanctuary in Switzerland (other members of his family group, including his ailing mother, had been allowed in). Levi had been arrested after a brief and (as he portrayed it) rather amateur few weeks as an antifascist partisan in the val d'Aosta. Of the 650 men, women and children crowded into the closed wagons of that train at Fossoli with De Benedetti and Levi, only twenty-four were to survive. De Benedetti's wife, separated from him on arrival in Auschwitz, was murdered by gas within hours, as were 525 others. De Benedetti and Levi were 'fortunate' (both used the word) to be selected for labour and transferred to Monowitz, where they were disinfected, tattooed and numbered, respectively, 174489 and 174517.

Every story of survival in Auschwitz is a story of extraordinary circumstance, of hard-fought infinitesimal advantage (an extra sip of watery soup, a matching pair of shoes, an hour out of the cold), rare reliance on others, and, above all, immense luck. Levi's and De Benedetti's stories are no exception. Even amongst fellow prisoners, Levi later wrote, the Italian Jews – the '174,000s' – were known as frail and naive, all lawyers and graduates, doomed in the crushing camp conditions of hard labour, violence and filth. Worse, De Benedetti was by all rights too old to survive here, even to be here at all. And he was never able to find work as a doctor, one of the (relatively) more comfortable and protected positions within the camp world. Yet, through force of character and through extraordinary good fortune – he had been selected for the gas chambers on four occasions, struck with swollen legs, unable to walk let alone work, only to be saved by prisoner-doctors – he was still alive in January 1945. Levi was fortunate in other ways, no less extraordinary: as we know from *If This is a Man* (1947), he found companionship in the resourceful Alberto (Dalla Volta), received precious scraps of food and support from Lorenzo (Perone), an Italian 'voluntary' labourer in the civilian workcamp attached to the Buna plant. Perhaps most remarkable of all, as he describes in *Moments of Reprieve* (1981), he fell sick with scarlet fever precisely as the Germans were evacuating the camp and leaving only the sick behind. His companion Alberto was not so 'lucky': he had immunity from a childhood bout of scarlet fever and so was taken on the infamous death march out of Auschwitz towards Germany. He never returned.

After liberation, survivors were moved into the main Auschwitz camp by the Soviets, and, from there, on to transit camps nearby. In March 1945, Levi and De Benedetti both reached the camp at Katowice, to the north of Auschwitz. As Levi recounts in his vivid second book, *The Truce* (1963), they would stay there, under the disorderly but humane control of the Russians, for nearly four months, waiting for the war to end and for some path homeward to open up amidst the devastation of postwar Europe and its millions of 'displaced persons'. De Benedetti set himself up as a highly popular camp doctor, and Levi offered himself – he was a 'doctor' of chemistry, after all – as his lab assistant and junior clerk. Towards the end of their time in Katowice, Levi fell gravely ill with pleurisy and De Benedetti's skill as both medic and blackmarketeer saved his life. Meanwhile, the Soviet authorities were undertaking a massive information-gathering exercise on Nazi crimes and they looked to survivors, doctors especially, for information on conditions in the concentration camps. At some point in the spring of 1945, then, De Benedetti and Levi drafted a short report on Auschwitz III for the Katowice Command.

After Katowice, De Benedetti shared in all the peregrinations and improvisations of Levi's journey home to Turin as described in *The Truce*. Their progress was a sort of baffling, picaresque reversal of the deportation journey of February 1944. They drifted east across Poland and into the USSR, looped north and then back south into Romania, west through Hungary, Austria, Germany, Austria again and, finally, south across the Brenner pass into northern Italy. By the time they reached Turin, in October 1945, the two were bound together as one, 'Leonardo and I', returning to life together, but also indelibly marked together by the horrors they had seen:

Late at night we crossed the Brenner, which we had passed in our exile twenty months before; our less tired companions celebrated with a cheerful uproar; Leonardo and I remained lost in a silence crowded with memories . . . how much had we lost, in those twenty months? What should we find at home? How much of ourselves had been eroded, extinguished? Were we returning richer or poorer, stronger or emptier? We did not know; but we knew that on the thresholds of our homes, for good or ill, a trial awaited us, and we anticipated it with fear. We felt in our veins the poison of Auschwitz, flowing together with our thin blood; where should we find the strength to begin our lives again? . . . We felt the weight of centuries on our shoulders . . . (*The Truce*)

Levi, the younger man, scarred by his experiences and prone to phases of depression, nevertheless seems to have reintegrated more quickly and more successfully than his older companion. He started working in a paint factory outside the city, met his future wife and, all the while, was telling stories, writing poems and fragments of prose. Over the course of 1946, these would come together as his first book – and, we now know, one of the very greatest works of Holocaust testimony – *If This is a Man*. De Benedetti was initially in deep shock and mourning for the loss of both his wife and his mother (who had died shortly after reaching Switzerland). It took the care of his family, and the friendship of Levi and others, to sustain him. Soon he took up work as a doctor in Turin. At some point in 1946, they had the idea of going back to their Katowice report and reworking it; and it was probably through De Benedetti that it found its way into the prominent, Turin-based medical journal, *Minerva Medica*. In the issue of 24 November 1946, in the original research section alongside articles on thrombosis, jaundice and brucellosis, we find: 'Dr Leonardo De Benedetti, Physician and Surgeon and Dr Primo Levi, Chemist, "Report On The Sanitary And Medical Organization Of The Monowitz Concentration Camp For Jews (Auschwitz – Upper Silesia)".' This is the remarkable document published here as *Auschwitz Report*.

Auschwitz Report

The report is a collaborative document, written, as the Italians say, 'four-handedly' (*a quattro mani*). There is little external evidence to suggest who wrote what, but we can speculate with some confidence on the basis of style, comparison with Levi's later works, and the distinct experiences and expertise of the two authors. Thus, De Benedetti must have been largely responsible for the strictly medical section detailing the six pathologies most prevalent in the camp (although the last category – 'work-related conditions' – draws on Levi's experience; see note 6 in the report) and perhaps also the description that follows of the workings of the infirmary at Monowitz. Levi's hand seems more apparent in the opening and closing parts, where we learn about the train journey and arrival, about living, eating and working conditions in Monowitz and, towards the end of the report, about the selections and the gas chambers at Auschwitz-Birkenau.[1]

The resulting 'four-hander' is a disturbing and compelling document, full of unexpected, often absurd detail and unfamiliar perspectives: we learn how bread, jam and cheese were distributed daily on the train convoy, but no water; how medical regimentation of triage was accompanied by queuing or running naked in the freezing snow; how gabardine raincoats were handed out to a lucky few for winter; and so on. There are telling examples of a Nazi obsession with appearances: the beds nearest to the door of a block are clean and ordered, but all the

---

1. The latter is an intriguing inclusion since, in *If This is a Man*, Levi famously chose to refer to the gas chambers only obliquely, reflecting the obscure shadow cast on Monowitz (where there were no gas chambers) by the fate that awaited those shipped to Birkenau.

others are filthy, infested and dust-ridden. Disinfections are routine and thorough, but meanwhile, the sick and the contagious live cramped together with the healthy: 'The rules of hygiene were completely ignored, apart from what little was necessary to keep up appearances.'

These and many other points of extraordinary detail aside, however, the larger significance of *Auschwitz Report* is threefold. First – and doubtless the reason most readers will pick up this book – there is simply the name of one of its authors. *Auschwitz Report* was Primo Levi's very first published piece of writing of any kind. In other words, one of the great voices of twentieth-century literature and testimony begins here. Such a 'first' would be extraordinary enough in and of itself, but the report also has more nuanced value for our understanding of Levi's work. As we have seen, Levi was working on the report in the same weeks and months that *If This is a Man* was taking shape. It is, in other words, a key element in what Levi's Italian editor, Marco Belpoliti, has called the 'laboratory' which produced that astonishing work. There are several direct lines of connection between the two: for example, the brief description of the October 1944 selections in the report feeds into the chapter 'October 1944' in *If This is a Man*; or the few lines at the end of the report about the days of limbo before liberation anticipate the dramatic diary sequence 'The Story of Ten Days' which ends *If This is a Man* (in fact, the first part of that book Levi wrote); and so on.

Where the report goes into more detail, we can do more interesting philological work. For example, the chapter 'Ka-Be' (for *Krankebau*, infirmary) in *If This is a Man* is a sustained reworking of the hospital sections of the report. Compare, for example, these two extracts:

> . . . a certain number of patients would be discharged every day, even if not completely recovered and still in a state of serious general debility; despite which they would have to start work again the following day. But those suffering from chronic diseases, or whose stay in hospital had lasted longer than a period of about two months, or who were readmitted too often due to relapses of their illness, were sent – as we have already reported in the case of those with tuberculosis, syphilis or malaria – to Birkenau and there eliminated in the gas chambers. (*Auschwitz Report*)

[The eight huts of 'Ka-Be'] . . . permanently hold a tenth of the population of the camp, but there are few who stay there longer than two weeks and none more than two months; within these limits they are held to die or be cured. Those who show signs of improvement are cared for in Ka-Be, those who seem to get worse are sent from Ka-Be to the gas chambers.[2] (*If This is a Man*)

In the transition from medical journal to book (always bearing in mind the dual authorship of the former), Levi takes enormous strides in the economy, rhythm and balance of his prose. Here we can literally see the characteristic style of *If This is a Man* being forged.

And questions of style are by no means incidental. Every reader of Levi has been struck by the apparent calm sobriety and rational control of his style, which seems to allow him to probe deeper into the void of Auschwitz than writers driven by (wholly understandable) resentment, confusion and lament. His is a still, small voice capable of transmitting to us, in some part, the 'evil tidings of what man's presumption made of man in Auschwitz' (*If This is a Man*).

2. Slightly adapted from the published translation.

11

Levi would later explain that style as having been modelled on the scientist's laboratory report, familiar from his professional life as a chemist. But it is perhaps rather *Auschwitz Report*, rooted in the 'scientific' presentation and analysis of medical data, that is the founding moment, the ur-document of that exceptional voice of reason. (And if this is so, De Benedetti deserves due recognition for his role in shaping that voice.) In broader terms, too, Levi's later role as a bridge between 'the two cultures' of literature and science (in books such as *The Periodic Table* or *The Sixth Day*) can be said to have its origin in *Auschwitz Report*.

At the same time, there is something more than dry professional science here, just as the stereotype of Levi's style as all clinical distance is inadequate. There are signs of the two authors, and perhaps particularly Levi, stretching the limits of medical pathology, reaching for the more varied and sensitive style that *If This is a Man* will achieve. There are touches of irony and sarcasm (the gas chambers are described, at one point, as the most radical of prophylactics), grotesque description, narrative suspense and psychological insight (such as in the tricking of the fearful deportees in Fossoli). Perhaps most striking of all is a recurrent pattern of structure and sequence, in which the report first describes an impression of working normality or near normality – the infirmary at Monowitz, for example, seems at first sight 'small, certainly, but complete in almost every department and efficiently run' – only then to skewer this impression on the appalling detail of the reality – the infirmary is in actual practice a place of mistreatment, neglect and meaningless regulation, of torture and violence meted out by its nurses. It is more akin to an antechamber of death than to a curing station.

Even without Levi's subsequent fame, *Auschwitz Report* would still constitute a fascinating historical document. It takes us back to a crucial moment in time for the Holocaust and for the entire history of postwar Europe; that is, the chaos and uncertainty of war's end. By Spring 1945, as *Auschwitz Report* and *If This is a Man* both indicate, much of the world already knew, through reports and images of the liberations of Belsen, Buchenwald and elsewhere, that something quite devastating and new had gone on in the Nazi camps. The stock images were already in place. But the hugely disproportionate number of Jewish victims was not yet clear or was downplayed, merged with the millions of others dead or displaced. It would take two decades or more for our current notion of the 'Holocaust' to emerge as a widely acknowledged, discrete and terrifyingly important event in twentieth-century history. The report, however, is strikingly, exceptionally clear on this, describing its subject-matter immediately as 'the annihilation of the European Jews' (Raul Hilberg's monumental 1961 history of these events would use a near-identical title, *The Destruction of the European Jews*). Like other survivors, De Benedetti and Levi were speaking, but not necessarily being heard.

This was a time of uncertainty in other respects also. No-one, perhaps especially not the survivors who had seen the camps from below and in conditions of extreme deprivation, knew the camp world in its every aspect. So, for example, De Benedetti and Levi describe the awful fate of the 'special command' – the *Sonderkommando*, charged with transferring the bodies from gas chambers to crematoria – but erroneously suggest they were made up of the worst criminal prisoners: in fact, the *Sonderkommandos* were, typically, young Jewish men, racial victims just like them. The report even gets one of its own authors wrong, when it says 'neither of the present writers were able to work in the hospital or in the chemical laboratory of the "Buna-Werke"'; Levi did, in fact, work in the Buna laboratory in the winter of 1944 (see note 3 to the report). Of course, even governments were getting facts wrong in 1945: the famous 'Soviet Extraordinary State Commission' report on Auschwitz (which this report may have fed into) came up with the figure of more than 4 million murdered in Auschwitz alone. Current estimates are around 1.6 million, 1.3 million of them Jews. These are the inevitable errors of early estimates and partial perspectives; to say nothing of political manipulation in the case of Stalin's Russia.

Another sign of the times comes in the touches of pro-Soviet rhetoric: we hear in passing of 'the unstoppable advance of the brave Russian troops', of the generosity of the camp liberators. This is perhaps unsurprising, given who commissioned the report, but it is nonetheless telling: Levi was never a communist (his partisan group was part of a liberal-socialist formation called 'Justice and Liberty'), but here (and later in *The Truce* also), the sense of gratitude to and even admiration for Soviet Russia is that of a generation which had much to be grateful to the Russians for.

Perhaps most resonant of all, however, is the

historical importance of the medicine itself. The Soviets had good reason to ask doctors to report on the Nazi camps. 'Medical' practice, from the eugenics and the 'euthanasia' programs of the 1930s to the infamous experiments of Josef Mengele, Eduard Wirths and others at Auschwitz (which are mentioned in passing in the report), held a very particular position within the Nazi project, a mark of its scientific modernity, its power and its danger. And the ghoulish stature taken on by Mengele, both in the camps – where he acquired the nickname 'Angel of Death' – and in popular culture after the war, is evidence of the great symbolic hold of medicine, of the 'doctor' and the 'healer', in our and perhaps all cultures. Medicine in Auschwitz has been probed from various angles over a long period; from the inside by testimonies such as Myklos Nyiszli's *Auschwitz. A Doctor's Eyewitness Account*, the memoir of a prisoner-doctor who assisted Mengele – a work Levi engages with in several intense pages of *The Drowned and the Saved* (1987) – or with a historian's eye in Robert Jay Lifton's *The Nazi Doctors*, which in turn inspired (along with Primo Levi) Martin Amis's novel *Time's Arrow*, an extraordinary dissection of the mind of a Nazi doctor, and his inversion of the Hippocratic oath to cure, not to injure. *Auschwitz Report*, with its more modest ambitions to chronicle everyday conditions of hygiene, sickness and treatment for the inmates at Auschwitz III, is like a missing piece in the mosaic of reflections probing the meanings and practices of Nazi medicine.

The final and most intensely human reason to read *Auschwitz Report* lies hidden between the lines, but is no less important for that. We know from Primo Levi's work – from his description of the bonds he forged with Alberto and Lorenzo; from Sandro, the taciturn hero of the story 'Iron' in *The Periodic Table*; or from the mournfully intimate reaction of so many of his readers when he died – that he was a man with a remarkable capacity for friendship. Whatever its larger literary or historical import, then, *Auschwitz Report* is also a document of the extraordinary friendship between Primo and 'Nardo,' forged in Fossoli, Monowitz and Katowice, and sustained for the rest of their lives. For most of forty years afterwards, they lived only a block apart in Turin. As Primo had supported Nardo through depression on their return, so Nardo would do the same during Primo's periodical lapses into depression (except for the last of these, in 1987, when Nardo was already dead). Primo, of course, grew into a famous writer, whereas Nardo did not write again about his experiences. He did, however, give talks and lectures and was at the heart of a network of former deportees, from Piedmont, elsewhere in Italy and abroad: on one occasion in the 1950s, Levi met Otto Frank, Anne Frank's father, at Nardo's apartment. And the two of them, in a sense, continued the work they had begun in the report by actively bearing witness together. In 1965, they visited Auschwitz together for official ceremonies and wrote a joint letter to the newspaper *La Stampa*, with fellow survivor–writer Giuliana Tedeschi. Both men gave depositions for the attempted extradition of Josef Mengele from Argentina, and, in 1971, for the trial of Friedrich Bosshammer, Adolf Eichmann's lieutenant in Italy. Both also gave extensive interviews to an oral history project of the 1980s recording the memories of Piedmontese camp survivors.[3] Like all good friends, the two had their fallings out also, notably when they disagreed about Israel's invasion of Lebanon in 1982. But there was the very deepest of bonds between them, hidden beneath the prose in

3. Levi's interview is in Primo Levi, *The Voice of Memory. Interviews 1961–87.* Cambridge: Polity Press, 2001, pp.218–49. The transcript of De Benedetti's interview is held in the deportee association (ANED) archive in Turin: I am grateful to Bruno Vasari, president of ANED and himself a survivor of Mauthausen, for permission to consult this document.

Minerva Medica but evident in the very story of its genesis. When Nardo died, in 1983 at the age of eighty-five, Levi wrote two moving memorial pieces (included here as a supplement to the report), capturing not only the duration and quality of their friendship, but also something of the exceptional human qualities of the friend and father-figure he had lost.

For what it tells us about Levi and the future work of this remarkable writer; for its status as a very particular historical document of the early reckoning with what we now call the Holocaust; and for its moving enactment of a lifelong friendship born in suffering; for all these reasons, *Auschwitz Report* feels like essential reading. Essential in the sense of necessary (it was Saul Bellow who first described a book of Levi's as 'necessary'); but essential also in that the report captures something of the essence of the concentration camp experience, reduced to a core of physiology and pathology. In his posthumously published collection *On The Natural History of Destruction*, W. G. Sebald – a writer whose work is shadowed by the Holocaust at every turn – contrasts certain over-wrought accounts of the Allied fire-bombings of German cities with what he calls the 'concrete memory' of contemporary medical reports. He mentions a 1945 document entitled 'Findings of Pathological and Anatomical Investigations After the Raids on Hamburg in 1943–45', and compares it to the diary of Michihiko Hachiya, a Hiroshima doctor. These, more than any literary elaborations, are the 'natural histories' of twentieth-century destruction; and the 'Report on the Sanitary and Medical Organization of the Monowitz Concentration Camp for Jews (Auschwitz – Upper Silesia)' belongs precisely in this company. Set against writings such as these, Sebald says, literary fiction 'knows nothing'; and, quoting Elias Canetti, 'If there were any point in wondering what form of literature is essential to a thinking, seeing human being today, then it is this'.

Robert S. C. Gordon

Biographical Note

Leonardo De Benedetti was born in Turin in 1898. He served in the medical corps in the Great War, spending six months in Murmansk in 1918, and graduated in medicine from Turin University in 1923. He worked as a general practitioner in a town outside Turin in the 1920s and 1930s. He married Jolanda Debenedetti in 1928. He lost his job in 1938 as a result of the Fascist anti-Semitic Racial Laws. In 1943, after trying to reach Switzerland, he was arrested and deported to Auschwitz. After the war, he worked as a doctor in Turin in various roles and was active in survivor circles. He died in October 1983, aged eighty-five.

Primo Levi was born in Turin in 1919. He graduated in chemistry from Turin University in

1941 and briefly lived in Milan. In 1943, he joined a partisan group but was arrested and deported to Auschwitz. He returned to Turin, married Lucia Morpurgo and began a career in industrial chemistry (and later management) that lasted until the mid-1970s. He published his first book, *If This is a Man*, in 1947. The book was republished in 1958, followed by (among others) *The Truce* (1963), *The Periodic Table* (1975), *The Wrench* (1978), *If Not Now, When?* (1982), *Other People's Trades* (1984) and *The Drowned and the Saved* (1987). He was also an occasional poet and translator. He became a prominent writer and speaker on the Holocaust and related issues, and his national and international reputation as a writer grew rapidly in the 1980s. He died in 1987, by suicide.

For further information on Levi (with some detail also on De Benedetti), see both Carole Angier, *The Double Bond. Primo Levi, A Biography*. London: Viking, 2002, and Ian Thomson, *Primo Levi. A Life*. London: Hutchinson, 2002.

Note on the Texts

1. *Auschwitz Report* was originally published as:
   Leonardo De Benedetti and Primo Levi, 'Rapporto sull'organizzazione igienico-sanitaria del campo di concentramento per ebrei di Monowitz (Auschwitz − Alta Silesia)', *Minerva Medica*, 35 / 2, n. 47, 24 November 1946, pp. 535–44.

   The report seems to have passed without notice and was, for all intents and purposes, forgotten. Only in 1993, after both authors had died, was it uncovered by the Turinese historian and critic Alberto Cavaglion and republished in the proceedings of a 1991 Turin conference (*Il ritorno dai Lager*, ed. Alberto Cavaglion. Milan: Franco Angeli, 1993, pp. 221–40). It was subsequently included in the 1997 edition of Levi's complete works

(Primo Levi, *Opere*, ed. Marco Belpoliti. Turin: Einaudi, 1997, vol. ii, pp. 1339–60). An Italian single-volume edition is currently in preparation.

2. The two articles by Levi on De Benedetti were originally published as follows:

Primo Levi, 'In Memory of a Good Man' as 'Ricordo di un uomo buono' in the Turin newspaper *La Stampa*, 21 October 1983.

Primo Levi, 'Leonardo De Benedetti' in the local Jewish community magazine *Ha Keillah*, December 1983.

The translations of the report and the two articles, as well as the notes and the glossary of medical terms, are by Judith Woolf.

Translator's Note

In working on this translation I have had to be attentive to two voices, that of a young man who would become a great writer, and that of a middle-aged one who would quietly return to being a good doctor, and whose professional expertise was essential to their joint testimony. The report which they wrote together was not intended as a piece of literature and nothing in it is a metaphor. Asked by the Soviet authorities to provide details of the sanitary and medical arrangements in the Monowitz Camp, they attempt to stick to their brief, but the language of medicine cracks and finally breaks down when confronted with the deliberate squalor and carelessly mocking brutality of what passed for medical services in this outpost of Auschwitz. I have tried to convey the tone and vocabulary of the original text, and I have also provided a glossary of medical and pharmaceutical terms for readers unfamiliar with oedema and phlegmons and the drugs which made up the inadequate pharmacopoeia of the Monowitz infirmary. These details matter, because they reveal the stark facts of a time and place in which human beings were condemned to die from diarrhoea and diphtheria and invasive ulcers as deliberately as they were condemned to die by gas.

Judith Woolf

Acknowledgements

The editor and translator wish to thank the following for their help and support in preparing this volume: Einaudi publishers and the Levi estate; the National Humanities Center, USA (John E. Sawyer Fellowship and Andrew W. Mellon Foundation); Marco Belpoliti, Alberto Cavaglion, John Foot, Marion and David Morris, Tom Penn, Bruno Vasari.

Report on the Sanitary and Medical Organization of the Monowitz Concentration Camp for Jews (Auschwitz — Upper Silesia)

Dr Leonardo De Benedetti, physician and surgeon
Dr Primo Levi, chemist

T HE PHOTOGRAPHIC EVIDENCE, and the already numerous accounts provided by ex-internees of the various concentration camps created by the Germans for the annihilation of the European Jews, mean that there is perhaps no longer anyone still unaware of the nature of those places of extermination and of the iniquities that were committed there. Nevertheless, in order to make better known the horrors of which we too were witnesses and very often victims throughout the course of a year, we believe that it will be useful to make public in Italy a report which we submitted to the government of the USSR on the request of the Russian Command of the concentration camp for Italian ex-prisoners at Katowice. We were inmates of this camp ourselves after our liberation by the Red Army towards the

31

end of January 1945. We have added some information of a general nature to the account given here, since our original report was required to concentrate exclusively on the operation of medical services in the Monowitz Camp. Similar reports were requested by the government in Moscow from all doctors, of whatever nationality, who had been liberated in the same way from other camps.

We left the concentration camp at Fossoli di Carpi (Modena) on 22 February 1944 with a convoy of 650 Jews of both sexes and all ages. The oldest was over eighty, the youngest a baby of three months. Many were ill, and some seriously so: an old man of seventy who had been struck down by a cerebral haemorrhage a few days before our departure was loaded onto the train anyway and died during the journey.

The train consisted simply of cattle trucks, locked on the outside; every wagon was crammed with over fifty people, the majority of whom had brought as much luggage with them as they could, because a German warrant officer attached to the Fossoli Camp had suggested to us, with the air of giving a piece of disinterested and kindly advice, that we should provide ourselves with plenty of warm clothes – jerseys, rugs, fur coats – because we were going to be taken to lands with a much harsher climate than our own. And he had added, with a benevolent little smile and a knowing wink, that if anyone had any hidden money or jewellery on them then it would be a good idea to take that along as well, since it would certainly come in useful up there. Most of those who were leaving had risen to the bait and followed a piece of advice which concealed a crude trap; others, a very few, preferred to entrust their belongings to some private citizen with free access to the Camp; while still others, whose arrest had not given them time to provide themselves with a change of clothing, left with only what they had on their backs.

The journey from Fossoli to Auschwitz lasted for exactly four days, and it was a very painful one, particularly on account of the cold, which was so intense, especially during the night, that in the morning the metal pipes which ran along the insides of the trucks would be found covered with ice due to the condensation of water vapour from the air we had breathed out. Another torment was thirst, which could not be quenched except with the snow that we gathered on the single daily halt, when the convoy would stop in open countryside and the passengers were allowed to get out of the trucks

under the strictest of surveillance from the numerous soldiers, ready, with their sub-machine-guns
constantly aimed, to open fire on anyone who
showed signs of moving away from the train.

It was during these brief halts that food was
distributed, truck by truck: bread, jam and cheese,
but never water or anything else to drink. The
possibility of sleep was reduced to a minimum, since
the quantity of suitcases and bundles cluttering the
floor did not allow anyone to settle into a comfortable position in which they could rest; instead, all
the passengers had to be content to crouch down as
best they could in a very small space. The floor of
the trucks was always soaking wet, and no provision
had been made to cover it even with a little straw.

As soon as the train reached Auschwitz (at about
9 p.m. on 26 February 1944) the trucks were
rapidly cleared by a number of SS men armed with
pistols and equipped with batons, and the passengers
were forced to leave their suitcases, bundles and
rugs alongside the train. The company was immediately divided into three groups: one of young and
apparently able-bodied men, comprising ninety-five
individuals; a second of women, also young – a
meagre group made up of only twenty-nine people –
and a third, the most numerous of all, of the

children, the infirm and the old. And, while the first two were sent separately to different camps, there is reason to believe that the third was taken straight to the gas chamber at Birkenau, and its members slaughtered that same evening.

The first group was taken to Monowitz, where there was a concentration camp administratively dependent on Auschwitz, and about 8 kilometres away from it, which had been set up towards the middle of 1942 in order to provide labour for the construction of the 'Buna-Werke' industrial complex, a subsidiary of IG Farbenindustrie. It housed ten to twelve thousand prisoners, even though its normal capacity was only seven to eight thousand men. The majority of these were Jews of every nationality in Europe, while a small minority was made up of German and Polish criminals, Polish 'politicals', and 'saboteurs'.

The 'Buna-Werke', intended for the production on a vast scale of synthetic rubber, synthetic gasoline, dyestuffs and other by-products of coal, occupied a rectangular area of about 35 square kilometres. One of the entrances to this industrial zone, completely surrounded by high barbed wire fences, was situated a few hundred metres from the Concentration Camp for Jews, and a short distance from this, and adjoining the periphery of the industrial zone, was a concentration camp for English prisoners of war, while further away there were other camps for civilian workers of various nationalities. We should add that the production cycle of the 'Buna-Werke' was never initiated; the starting date, originally fixed for August 1944, was repeatedly postponed because of air raids and sabotage by Polish civilian workers, right up to the evacuation of the district by the German army.

Monowitz was therefore a typical 'Arbeits-Lager'. Every morning, the entire population of the Camp – apart from the sick and the small labour force assigned to internal work – would file out in perfect ranks, to the sound of a band playing military marches and cheerful popular songs, to reach their places of work, up to six or seven kilometres distant for some squads. The route would be covered at a rapid pace, almost at a run. Before the departure for work, and after returning from it, the daily ceremony of the roll-call would take place in a special square in the Lager, where all the prisoners had to stand in rigid formation, for between one and three hours, whatever the weather.

As soon as they arrived at the Camp, the group of ninety-five men was taken to the disinfection unit, where all of its members were immediately made to undress and then subjected to a total and painstaking depilation: head hair, beards and all other hair quickly fell away beneath scissors, razors and clippers. After which they were put into the shower room and locked up there until the following morning. Tired, hungry, thirsty, half asleep, amazed by what they had already seen and worried about their immediate future, but anxious above all about the fate of the dear ones from whom they had been suddenly and brutally separated a few hours earlier, with their minds tormented by sombre and tragic forebodings, they had to spend the whole night standing up, with their feet in the water that trickled from the pipes and ran over the floor. Finally, at about six the following morning, they were subjected to a complete rub-down with a solution of Lysol[1] and then to a hot shower; after which the Camp clothes were handed out, and they were sent to get dressed in another large room, which they had to reach from the outside of the building, going out naked into the snow with their bodies still wet from their recent shower.

The winter outfit of the Monowitz prisoners consisted of a jacket, a pair of trousers, a cap and an

---

1. Medical and pharmaceutical terms are explained in the Glossary.

overcoat of woollen cloth in broad stripes, plus a
shirt, a pair of cotton underpants and a pair of foot-
cloths, a pullover and a pair of boots with wooden
soles. Many of the foot-cloths and the underpants
had obviously been made out of the 'tallit' – the
sacred shawl with which Jews cover themselves
during prayers – retrieved from the luggage of
some of the deportees and made use of in this
way as a mark of contempt.

By the month of April, when the cold, though less
severe, had not yet gone, the thick clothing and
pullovers would be withdrawn and trousers and
jackets replaced by similar articles in cotton, also
with broad stripes; and only towards the end of
October would the winter garments be distributed
again. However, this no longer happened in the
autumn of 1944 because the woollen suits and coats
had reached the end of any possibility of reuse, so
the prisoners had to face the winter of 1944–45
dressed in the same thin clothes as during the
summer months, with only a small minority being
given a light gabardine raincoat or a pullover.

Having spare clothes or underwear was strictly
forbidden, so it was practically impossible to wash
shirts or underpants; these items were officially
changed at intervals of thirty, forty or fifty days,

depending on availability and without the possibility of choice. The new underwear was not actually clean, of course, but simply disinfected by steam, because there was no laundry in the Camp. It usually consisted of short cotton underpants and of shirts: always cotton or some other thin cloth, often without sleeves, always of a disgusting appearance because of the many stains of all kinds, and often reduced to rags. Sometimes instead one would be given the jacket or trousers from a pair of pyjamas, or even some article of female underwear. The repeated disinfections weakened the fibres of the cloth, removing all resistance to wear and tear. All this material represented the shoddiest part of the linen seized from the members of the various transports which, as is common knowledge, flooded ceaselessly into the station at Auschwitz from every part of Europe. Coats, jackets and trousers, whether summer or winter, were distributed in an unbelievably bad condition, covered with patches and impregnated with filth (mud, machine oil, paint). The prisoners were personally obliged to see to repairs, although they were not provided with either needles or thread. Permission for an exchange was obtained with extreme difficulty, and only when any attempt at repair was clearly impossible. Foot-cloths could not be exchanged at all, and their replacement was left to the initiative of each individual. It was forbidden to own a handkerchief, or indeed a scrap of cloth of any kind.

The boots were made in a special workshop inside the Camp; the wooden soles were nailed to uppers of leather, leatherette, or cloth and rubber, taken from the shoddiest of the footwear obtained from incoming convoys. When they were in good condition they provided reasonable protection against the cold and the wet, but they were completely unsuitable for marches, however short, and were the cause of epidermal ulcers of the feet. Anyone in possession of boots that were the right size and a matching pair could count himself lucky. When they deteriorated they were repaired innumerable times, beyond any reasonable limit, so new footwear was very rarely seen, and the sort usually handed out did not last for more than a week. Bootlaces were not distributed and substitutes were contrived by each individual from twisted paper cord, or from electric flex when it was possible to find any.

Hygienic and sanitary conditions in the Camp actually appeared at first sight to be good: the paths and avenues that separated the various 'blocks' were well-maintained and clean, in so far as the mud of the road surface permitted; the outsides of the 'blocks' were of well-painted wood, and the insides had floors diligently swept and washed every morning, with the three-storey bunks, the so-called 'castles', perfectly aligned and the blankets on the pallets completely flat and smooth. But all this was only the outward appearance, the reality was very different; in fact the 'blocks', which should normally have housed 150 to 170 people, were always crammed with not less than 200, and often as many as 250, so that two people had to sleep in almost every bed. In these conditions, the cubic capacity of the dormitory was certainly less than the minimum needed for respiration and oxygenation of the blood. The pallets consisted of a sort of palliasse more or less filled with wood-shavings, reduced almost to dust from long use, and of two blankets. Apart from the fact that these were never changed, and not subjected, except very rarely and for exceptional reasons, to any disinfection, they were mostly in a dreadful state: threadbare from very long use, torn and covered in stains of every kind. Only the pallets most in view were provided with more decent covers, almost clean and sometimes even attractive; these were the pallets on the lower tiers and nearest the entrance door.

Naturally these beds were reserved for the minor 'hierarchs' of the Camp: the squad Kapos and their assistants, the aides of the block Kapo, or simply the friends of the one or the other.

This explains the impression of cleanliness, order and hygiene which greeted anyone entering a dormitory for the first time and giving the inside a superficial glance. In the structure of the 'castles', the supporting beams and the planks on which the pallets rested, lived thousands of bed bugs and fleas which gave the prisoners sleepless nights; nor were the disinfections of the dormitories with nitrogen mustard vapour,[2] which were carried out every three or four months, sufficient for the destruction of these guests, which continued to vegetate and multiply almost undisturbed.

Against lice, on the other hand, a war to the death was waged in order to avert the onset of an epidemic of petechial typhus; every evening on returning from work, and with greater strictness on Saturday afternoons (devoted, among other things, to the shaving of heads and beards, and sometimes also of body hair) the so-called 'louse inspection' would be carried out. Every prisoner had to strip and subject

2. Nitrogen mustard: a highly lethal poison gas developed in Germany during World War II as a chemical weapon, although it was never used in action.

his garments to a meticulous examination by the specially appointed inspectors, and if even a single louse was found on a deportee's shirt, all the personal clothing of every inmate of the dormitory was immediately despatched to be disinfected, and the men were subjected to a shower, preceded by a rub-down with Lysol. They then had to spend the entire night naked, until their clothes were brought back from the disinfection hut in the early hours of the morning, soaking wet.

However, no other prophylactic measures were put in place against infectious diseases, even though there was no shortage of these: typhus and scarlet fever, diphtheria and chickenpox, measles, erysipelas, etcetera, not counting the numerous skin infections, such as tineas, impetigo and scabies. It is quite astonishing, given such disregard for the rules of hygiene and with people living in such close proximity, that rapidly spreading epidemics never broke out.

One of the greatest risk factors for the transmission of infectious diseases was represented by the fact that a significant percentage of prisoners were not provided with a mess tin or a spoon; consequently three or four people in succession would be forced to eat from the same container or with the same implement, without having had the chance to wash it.

The food, inadequate in quantity, was of inferior quality. It consisted of three meals: in the morning, straight after reveille, 350 grams of bread would be distributed on four days of the week and 700 grams on the other three, giving a daily average of 500 grams – an amount which would have been fairly reasonable if the bread itself had not indisputably contained a very large quantity of dross, amongst which sawdust was much in evidence; also in the mornings there would be 25 grams of margarine with about 20 grams of sausage or a spoonful of jam or soft cheese. The margarine was distributed on six days of the week only, and later this was reduced to three. At noon the deportees received a litre of turnip or cabbage soup, completely tasteless due to the absence of any kind of flavouring, and every evening after work a further litre of a slightly thicker soup with a few potatoes or now and then some peas and chickpeas, but this too was completely devoid of any fat to flavour it. One might infrequently find a few shreds of meat. To drink, half a litre of ersatz coffee, without sugar, was distributed morning and evening; only on Sundays was it sweetened with saccharin. There was no drinking water at Monowitz; the running water in the washrooms could only be put to external use, since it was river water, which arrived at the Camp neither filtered nor sterilized and was therefore highly dubious. It was clear in appearance, but of a yellowish colour if seen in any depth; its taste was between the metallic and the sulphurous.

The prisoners were required to take a shower two or three times a week. However, these ablutions were not sufficient to keep them clean as soap was handed out in very parsimonious quantities: only a single 50-gram bar per month. Its quality was extremely poor; it consisted of a rectangular block, very hard, devoid of any fatty material but instead full of sand. It did not produce lather and disintegrated very easily, so that after a couple of showers it was completely used up. After showering, there was no way of rubbing down one's body or of drying it since there were no towels, and on coming out of the bath-house one had to run naked, whatever the time of year, the atmospheric and meteorological conditions or the temperature, as far as one's own particular 'block', where one's clothes had been left.

The work to which the great majority of prisoners was assigned was manual labour of various kinds, all very demanding and unsuited to the physical condition and the abilities of those condemned to it; very few were employed in work which had any connection with the profession or trade they had practised in civilian life. Thus, neither of the present writers were able to work in the hospital or in the chemical laboratory of the 'Buna-Werke',[3] but were forced to share the lot of their companions and undergo labours beyond their strength, sometimes working as navvies with pick and shovel, sometimes unloading coal or sacks of cement, or doing other sorts of very heavy work, all of which naturally took place out of doors, winter and summer, in snow, rain, sun or wind, and without clothing that provided adequate protection against low temperatures or bad weather. This kind of work, moreover, always had to be carried out at the double and without any breaks except for an hour, from noon till one, for the midday meal; woe betide anyone who was caught being inactive or standing at ease during working hours.

3. This paragraph appears to have been written by De Benedetti, who was clearly unaware that Levi had worked as a laboratory technician in the Buna factory during the winter of 1944, as he describes in *If This is a Man*. This misunderstanding on De Benedetti's part is probably due to the fact that most of the so-called 'Chemical Commando' continued to do heavy manual labour, as did Levi himself during his first nine months as a member of it.

From the brief account we have given of living conditions in the Monowitz Concentration Camp, it is easy to deduce the diseases which most frequently affected the prisoners, along with their causes. They can be divided into the following groups:

1) dystrophic diseases
2) diseases of the gastrointestinal apparatus
3) diseases due to cold
4) infective diseases, general and cutaneous
5) conditions requiring surgery
6) work-related conditions

Dystrophic diseases – The diet, which as we have seen was much inferior to what was required from a quantitative point of view, was lacking from a qualitative one in two important respects: it was deficient, that is to say, in fats, and especially in animal protein, apart from those miserable 20–25 grams of sausage that were administered two or three times a week. It was also lacking in vitamins. It is clear, therefore, that nutritional deficiencies of these kinds and on this scale were the primary cause of the dystrophies that affected almost all of the prisoners from their first weeks as inmates. All of them, in fact, very quickly became emaciated, and the majority of them presented with oedemas, particularly localized to the lower limbs, although oedemas of the face were also present. These dystrophies can also be held responsible for the ease with which various infections were contracted, especially those affecting the integrity of the skin, and for their tendency to become chronic. Thus, certain epidermal ulcers of the feet, directly caused by the footwear, which was anti-physiological in shape and size; boils, which were very frequent and numerous in the same subject; the equally frequent leg ulcers; phlegmons, etcetera, would not show any tendency to heal but would turn into turbid sores with a lardaceous base and continual sero-purulent suppuration, and sometimes with an abundance of yellowish-grey granulomas which were not ameliorated even by painting with silver nitrate. And finally, the diarrhoea that affected almost all of the deportees can also be attributed, to a significant extent, to alimentary dystrophy. This explains why the deportees rapidly lost their strength, since the disappearance of subcutaneous fat was accompanied by the onset of considerable atrophy of the muscular tissue.

At this point we need to mention vitamins. From what we have reported so far, it might seem obvious that vitamin deficiency syndromes – particularly from the lack of Vitamins C and B – would be common. On the contrary, as far as we are aware cases of scurvy or polyneuritis did not occur, at least in a typical and fully developed form, and we believe this to be due to the fact that the average life expectancy of the majority of prisoners was too short for the body to have time to display obvious clinical symptoms of suffering from the lack of those vitamins.

Diseases of the gastrointestinal apparatus – We will pass over those diseases, by which many prisoners were affected, which were not directly caused by living conditions in the Camp, such as low or high stomach acid, gastroduodenal ulcers, appendicitis, inflammation of the bowel, diseases of the liver. We will note only that these pathological conditions, pre-existent in many deportees before their arrival at Monowitz, became aggravated, or underwent relapses if previously cured. What we particularly want to discuss here is the diarrhoea to which we have already referred in the previous paragraph, both because of its prevalence and because of the gravity of its course, in many cases rapidly fatal. It usually erupted suddenly, sometimes preceded by dyspeptic disturbances, as a result of some immediate cause that represented the accidental determining factor, such as, for example, a prolonged exposure to cold or the consumption of food which had gone bad (sometimes the bread was mouldy) or which was difficult to digest. It is worth mentioning in this connection that many prisoners, to relieve the pangs of hunger, would eat potato peelings, raw cabbage leaves or rotten potatoes or turnips which they collected from amongst the kitchen refuse. However, it is probable that there were many other causal factors in serious cases of diarrhoea, and two interdependent ones in particular: chronic dyspepsia and the resulting dystrophy due to malnutrition. Those affected presented with numerous evacuations of the bowels – from a minimum of five or six up to twenty or even more a day – liquid and with a great deal of mucus, sometimes accompanied by blood, and preceded and accompanied by acute abdominal pain. The appetite might be preserved, but in many cases the patients presented with persistent anorexia, so that they refused to take any nourishment; these were the most serious cases, which rapidly developed towards a fatal outcome. There was invariably a very intense thirst. If the condition showed a tendency towards recovery, the number of evacuations diminished, becoming reduced to two or three a day, while the consistency of the faeces altered, becoming less liquid. From these bouts of diarrhoea the patients always emerged in poor condition, with a considerable worsening of their general state of health and a more pronounced appearance of emaciation due to the significant dehydration of the tissues.

The standardized treatment[4] was two-fold: nutritional and medicinal. Having been admitted to hospital, the patients were subjected to a total fast for a period of twenty-four hours, after which they were given a special diet until their condition had decidedly improved: that is, until the number of evacuations having diminished and the faeces having become more formed, the prognosis of their illness had become clearly favourable. This dietary regime consisted in the suspension of the sausage ration and the midday soup; black bread was replaced by white and the evening soup by sweetened semolina, reasonably thick. In addition, the doctors advised the patients to drink little liquid, or preferably not to drink at all, although the quantity of morning and evening coffee was not officially reduced. Medicinal

4. 'La cura, standardizzata': there is an important, if unobtrusive, distinction here between the 'standard treatment' which patients would receive in a normal hospital and the parody of medical care which was 'standardized' in the Monowitz infirmary.

treatment was based on the administration of three or four albumin tannate tablets and the same number of charcoal tablets *pro die*; in the most serious cases, the patients also received five drops (!) of tincture of opium together with a few drops of Cardiazol.

Diseases due to cold – The daily prolonged exposure to the cold and to harsh weather, against which the prisoners were not protected in any way, and to the wet, explains the frequency of rheumatic conditions affecting the respiratory system and the joints, of neuralgias and of frostbite.

Bronchitis, pneumonia and broncho-pneumonia were, so to speak, the order of the day even during the summer, but naturally they were particularly rampant during the winter, autumn and spring. Treatment was extremely basic: cold compresses on the chest, a few antipyretic tablets and, in the most serious cases, sulphonamides in totally inadequate doses, along with a little Cardiazol. For neuralgias – lumbago and sciatica were especially common – and for arthritis the patients were subjected to heat treatment; no treatment was practised for frostbite apart from amputation of the affected part when the frostbite was sufficiently severe.

Infectious diseases – The exanthemata represented the most common of these, especially scarlet fever, chickenpox, erysipelas and diphtheria. Cases of abdominal typhus also occurred from time to time. Anyone who came down with one of these diseases would be admitted to an isolation ward, but in an indiscriminate way: without, that is, there being any separation between patients with different kinds of infection. Consequently it was very easy for a patient who had been admitted to the infirmary with one infectious disease to contract another there through contagion, especially since neither the blankets on the beds nor the bowls in which the soup was distributed were ever disinfected. Scarlet fever and erysipelas were combatted with sulphonamides – always administered, however, in reduced doses; diphtheria cases were left to themselves due to the total lack of serum, and their treatment was limited to gargling with a very dilute solution of Chinosol and to the administration of a few Panflavin lozenges. Understandably, the death rate for diphtheria was 100 per cent, since any patients who managed to survive the acute phase succumbed later to cardiac arrest, either because of some further complication or because they also came down with another contagious disease.

As to syphilis, tuberculosis and malaria, we are not able to give any data as to their frequency since the syphilitic, the tubercular and the malarial – the latter even if long since cured and accidentally found out through their own incautious confession – were immediately dispatched to Birkenau and eliminated there in the gas chambers. It cannot be denied that this was a radical prophylactic method!

Skin infections of every kind were very prevalent, but especially boils and abscesses – which, as we have already said, always had a very protracted course, subject to relapses and with many concurrent sites – as well as sycosis of the beard area and tineas. Against the former, only surgical treatment by incision and drainage was carried out, since there was no possibility of practising fever therapy by means of vaccine or drug treatment; although, in the most persistent cases, the patients were subjected to autohemotherapy. Against the latter – sycosis and tineas – there were no specific remedies, and in particular no iodine. The sufferers' faces were plastered with one or another of the available ointments, with less than no therapeutic effect. In the light of the ever greater prevalence of these skin diseases, on the one hand such prophylactic measures as a ban on patients having their beards shaved, to prevent the transmission of infection by razors and shaving-brushes, were finally adopted, while on the other, steps were taken to intensify treatment by subjecting the patients to ultraviolet radiation. The most serious cases of sycosis were temporarily transferred to the hospital at Auschwitz to undergo X-ray therapy.

On the subject of skin conditions, we must once again mention the prevalence of scabies, which was treated with a daily rub-down with Mitigal in a special ward to which patients were admitted only in the evenings, spending the nights there while having to continue working during the day in the squad to which they were normally attached. In other words, there was no special 'Commando' for scabies sufferers to which those infested were assigned for the duration of their condition; so, since they continued to work in the midst of individuals who had not yet been infested, contagion was very frequent, due to the shared use of tools and to living in close proximity.

Conditions requiring surgery – Once again we do not wish to dwell on conditions requiring surgical inter-vention which were not causally connected to living conditions in the Camp. We will simply report that even major surgery was regularly performed, mostly abdominal, such as partial gastrectomy and pyloroplasty for gastroduodenal ulcers, appendectomies, rib resections for empyema, etcetera; as well as orthopaedic interventions for fractures and dislocations. If the general condition of the patient did not offer sufficient guarantee of resistance to the trauma of surgery, he would be given a blood transfusion before the operation; this was also done to combat secondary anaemia and serious haemorrhages caused by gastric ulcers or accidental trauma. For donors, recourse was had to recently arrived deportees who were still in good general shape; blood donation was voluntary and the donor was rewarded with a fortnight's rest in hospital, during which time he received special rations. For this reason, offers of blood were always very numerous.

We have no reason to suppose – indeed, we believe that we can rule it out – that operations for the purpose of scientific research were performed in the Monowitz hospital, as they were on a vast scale in other concentration camps. We know, for example, that at Auschwitz a section of the hospital was used for research into the effects of castration followed by cross-gender grafting of the reproductive glands.[5]

5. i.e., 'scientific experiments' involving transplanting ovaries into men and testes into women.

The operating theatre was reasonably well equipped, in so far as was necessary for the procedures carried out there. The walls were covered in washable white tiles; there was an adjustable operating table, of a rather old-fashioned type but still in good condition, which allowed the patient to be placed in the main operative positions, and an electric sterilizer for surgical instruments; illumination was provided by several movable lamps and a large, fixed, central light. On one wall, behind a wooden screen, wash-basins with hot and cold running water were installed so that the surgeon and his assistants could scrub their hands.

On the subject of aseptic surgery, we should add that hernias were also regularly operated on at the request of the patient, at least until the middle of spring 1944; from then on these operations were discontinued – apart from very exceptional cases of strangulated hernia – even when it was a question of very large hernias that were really an impediment to work. This decision was taken on the supposition that patients might submit themselves to the operation in order to get a month's rest in hospital.

The most frequent operations were for phlegmons, and were carried out in a theatre set aside for surgery dealing with septic conditions. Phlegmons, along with diarrhoea, constituted one of the most important chapters in the characteristic pathology of the concentration camp. They were mainly localized on the lower limbs, more rarely having their site in some other part of the body. As a rule, it was possible to identify their starting-point in cutaneous lesions of the feet, caused by the footwear: ulcers, originally superficial and of limited extent, which became infected and spread, with locally extending infiltration, either peripheral or in depth, or giving rise to metastatic infiltration at a distance. At times, though, it was not possible to determine the point of entry of the pathogenic micro-organisms, the infiltration of the soft tissue having developed without it being possible to detect any cutaneous lesion in its vicinity or at a distance; this was probably due to a localization of micro-organisms originating in some focus from which they had been transferred via the bloodstream. Patients were operated on without delay, with numerous ample incisions; however, the subsequent development of the lesions was always very lengthy and, even when suppuration was coming to an end, the incisions did not show any tendency to scar over. Post-operative treatment consisted simply in drainage of the surgical wound; no treatment was put into effect to stimulate the body's own defences. Relapses were therefore very likely, often leading to a succession of operations on the same individual to open and drain the sacs of pus that formed at the periphery of the previous incisions. When eventually the healing process appeared to have reached a satisfactory stage, patients would be discharged from hospital and sent back to work even though their wounds had not yet completely healed, and subsequent treatment was carried out on an out-patient basis. It stands to reason that the majority of those discharged in this way had to return to hospital after a few days, either because of local relapses or due to the development of new foci in other sites.

Also very common was acute otitis, which led to a particularly high percentage of mastoid complications; these too were routinely operated on by the otorhinolaryngologist.

The treatment of skin infections was based on the use of four ointments, which were applied successively in a standardized way, depending on the stage of the lesions. Firstly, at the infiltration stage, the lesion and the surrounding skin were covered with Ichthyol ointment to reduce swelling; later, once the formation of pus had occurred and the focus had been opened, its base was covered with Collargol ointment as a disinfectant; once the suppuration had ceased or greatly diminished, Pellidol ointment was used to stimulate scarring, followed by another of zinc oxide to aid epithelialization.

Work-related conditions – Given the very high rate of employment in manual labour, specific occupational diseases were not really in evidence apart from accidental injuries requiring surgery, such as contusions, fractures and dislocations; but we can report on one case which is known to us.

At a certain period – August 1944 – the men attached to the so-called 'Chemical Commando' were employed in reorganizing a storeroom containing sacks of a substance of a phenolic nature. From the very first day of work, this substance, in the form of fine powder, stuck to the faces and hands of the labourers, held there by their sweat; subsequent exposure to the sun caused, in all of them, first a strong pigmentation of the exposed areas, accompanied by intense burning, and then an extensive desquamation in large flakes. Even though the new layer of skin that was thus exposed to the contaminating agent was particularly sensitive and painful, the work continued for three weeks without any protective measures being adopted. And even though all of the men in the above-mentioned

Commando – about fifty of them – were affected by this painful dermatitis, none of them was admitted to hospital.[6]

Having given this survey of the most common diseases in the Monowitz Camp and of their causes, we are forced to admit that we are unable to give precise data on their frequency in absolute and relative terms, since neither of us ever had the chance to enter the hospital except as a patient. What we have written so far, and what we still have to say, is the fruit of everyday observation and of the information which we gleaned more or less accidentally while conversing with our companions and with doctors and infirmary staff with whom we were on terms of familiarity or friendship.

The Camp hospital was set up only a few months before our arrival at Monowitz, which took place towards the end of February 1944. Before that period there were no medical services and the sick had no possibility of getting treatment, but were forced to labour as usual every day until they collapsed from exhaustion at their work. Naturally,

6. Levi describes the same episode in *If This is a Man*: 'We are the chemists, "therefore" we work at the phenylbeta sacks . . . The phenylbeta seeped under our clothes and stuck to our sweating limbs and chafed us like leprosy; the skin came off our faces in large burnt patches.'

such cases occurred with great frequency. Confirmation of death would then be carried out in a singular fashion; the task was entrusted to two individuals, not doctors, who were armed with ox sinews and had to beat the fallen man for several minutes on end. After they had finished, if he failed to react with some movement, he was considered to be dead, and his body was immediately taken to the crematorium. If, on the contrary, he moved, it signified that he was not dead after all, so he would be forced to resume his interrupted work.

Later on, the basic nucleus of a medical service was established with the setting up of an out-patient clinic, where anyone who felt ill could present himself for a medical examination; although if someone was not recognized as ill by the doctors, he would immediately receive severe corporal punishment from the SS. Otherwise, if his condition was judged to be such as to prevent him from working, he would be granted a few days' rest. Later still, a few blocks were set aside for use as an infirmary, which gradually expanded with the setting up of additional services; so that, during our stay in the Camp, the following were in operation:

- out-patient clinic for general medicine
- out-patient clinic for general surgery
- otorhinolaryngology and ophthalmology out-patient clinic
- dental surgery (in which fillings and the most basic prosthetic work were also carried out)
- ward for infective surgical cases
- general clinical ward, with a section for nervous and mental illnesses, equipped with a small electric shock therapy apparatus
- ward for infectious diseases and diarrhoea
- recuperation ward – 'Schonungs-Block' – to which were admitted dystrophic and oede-matous patients and certain convalescents
- physiotherapy surgery, with a quartz lamp for ultraviolet radiation and lamps for infra-red radiation
- chemical, bacteriological and serological re-search unit

There were no X-ray machines, so if an X-ray examination was needed the patient would be dis-patched to Auschwitz, where there was good X-ray equipment, and from where he would return with a radiological diagnosis.

This description might suggest a hospital which

was small, certainly, but complete in almost every department and efficiently run; but in reality there were many deficiencies, some of which, such as the lack of drugs and the shortage of medical equipment, were perhaps insurmountable, given the grave situation in which Germany already found herself, under pressure on one side from the unstoppable advance of the brave Russian troops and on the other from daily air raids by the heroic Anglo-American air force; but others could have been remedied, had there been the will to do so, by better organization of services.

The first and most important of these deficiencies was the inadequacy in number and capacity of the facilities. For example, there was no waiting-room for the clinics, so patients reporting to them were forced to stay out of doors – awaiting their turn in endless queues, whatever the season and whatever the weather – when, already exhausted from their long working day, they returned to the Camp in the evening, since the out-patient facilities were only in operation after all the labourers had returned to the Camp and the evening roll-call was over. Before entering the clinics, every patient had to take off his shoes, and was therefore forced to walk with bare feet over floors, such as that of the surgical out-patient clinic, which were very dirty due to the presence of soiled dressings thrown on the ground, and consequently soiled with blood and pus.

In the wards, there was a very serious shortage in the number of beds, which made it necessary for every pallet to be used by two people, whatever the nature and the gravity of the disease from which they were suffering; the possibility of contagion was therefore very high, especially considering the fact that, due to the lack of shirts, the hospital patients went naked; indeed, on entry to the hospital, every patient would deposit all his clothes in the disinfection unit. The blankets and palliasses of the pallets were absolutely filthy, stained with blood and pus and often with faeces, which patients in a pre-agonal state would void involuntarily.

The rules of hygiene were completely ignored, apart from what little was necessary to keep up appearances. So, for example, due to a shortage of mess tins, meals would be served in two or three shifts, and the patients in the second or third shift would be forced to eat their soup from receptacles inadequately rinsed in a bucket of cold water. In the so-called 'Schonungs-Block', running water had not been plumbed in, which was indeed also the case in all the other wards; but while the inmates of the latter were able to go to a specially designated 'Waschraum' to wash themselves whenever they wanted, those admitted to the former were only able to avail themselves of the chance to wash once a day, in the morning, over two hundred of them sharing six basins into which the nurses would occasionally pour a litre of water from tubs brought in for this purpose from outside. In this same ward, the bread would be brought in from the dressing station, where it had been left the previous evening on a bench which, during the day, served the patients as a stool on which to prop their feet while their dressings were being changed, after which it was always smeared with blood and pus that would then be hastily wiped off with a rag soaked in cold water.

In order to be allowed into the hospital, the patients judged by the clinic doctors to be worthy of admission had to report a second time the following morning, immediately after reveille, to undergo another, very cursory examination by the doctor in charge of medical services; if he confirmed the need for hospitalization, they would be sent to the shower room. There they would be shaved to the last hair, then made to take a shower, and finally they would be sent to the relevant section of the hospital. To get there, they would have to go outside, covered only by a wrap, and walk a hundred to two hundred metres in this state, whatever the season and whatever the atmospheric and meteorological conditions.

In the various clinical wards, the doctor in charge, assisted by one or two nurses, would perform his morning round without personally going up to the patients' beds; rather, it was they who would have to get out of bed and go to him, excluding only those who were completely prevented from doing so by the seriousness of their condition. In the evenings, there would be a rapid follow-up examination.

In the surgical wards, the dressings would be applied in the mornings, and since the dormitory was divided into three aisles and each aisle was treated in turn, it followed that each patient received treatment only every third day. The dressings were secured with paper bandages which tore and came apart in the course of a few hours; so the wounds, whether septic or not, were always left exposed. Only in rare and exceptional cases would dressings be secured with adhesive plaster, which was used with the utmost frugality on account of its scarcity.

Medication was reduced to a minimum; many

products, even the most basic and commonly used, were totally absent, while of others there was only a meagre amount. There was a little aspirin, a little Pyramidon, a little Prontosil (the only representative of the sulphonamides), a little sodium bicarbonate, a few phials of Coramine and caffeine. There was no camphorated oil, no strychnine, no opium or any of its derivatives apart from a small quantity of tincture; there was no belladonna or atropine; there was no insulin, no expectorants, nor yet salts of bismuth or Epsom salts, pepsin or hydrochloric acid; while the purgatives and laxatives were represented only by Purgatin. However there were reasonable quantities of hexamethylenetetramine, of medicinal charcoal and of albumin tannate. Also missing were phials of calcium and of any preparation which would act as a tonic. There was a reasonable quantity of soluble evipal for intravenous use and of phials of ethyl chloride for anaesthesia; the latter was widely used even for minor interventions, such as lancing a boil.

Every so often, the dispensary was given new blood by the receipt, on the arrival of new convoys of prisoners, of various quantities of the most disparate products and the most diverse proprietary drugs – many of them useless – discovered in the luggage confiscated from the new arrivals; but all in all, requirements were always far in excess of supply.

The staff were recruited entirely from among the deportees themselves. The doctors were chosen, subject to examination, from among those who had declared on entering the Camp that they had a degree in medicine, with priority going to those who were fluent in German or Polish. Their services were rewarded with improved rations and better clothing and footwear. The orderlies and nurses, on the other hand, were picked without any criterion of previous professional experience; for the most part they were striking physical specimens who had obtained their positions – naturally very much sought after – thanks to their friendships and connections with doctors already in post, or with members of the hierarchy of the Camp. It followed that, while the doctors, on the whole, displayed a reasonable competence and a certain degree of civility, the auxiliary staff distinguished themselves by their ignorance of, or contempt for, every hygienic, therapeutic and humanitarian principle; they went so far as to barter part of the soup and bread intended for the patients in exchange for cigarettes, items of clothing and other such things. The patients were often beaten for trivial offences; the distribution of rations took place in an irregular way, and when it came to prisoners who were found guilty of more serious faults – such as stealing bread from their companions – the customary punishment was the immediate expulsion of the culprit from the hospital, and his immediate return to work, preceded by the administration of a certain number of blows (usually twenty-five) to the back, delivered very energetically with a tube of rubberized cloth. Another type of punishment was being forced to spend a quarter of an hour on a rather high stool with a very narrow seat, balancing on tip-toe, with the legs bent at the knees and hips and the arms held out horizontally in front at shoulder height. Usually the patient would lose his balance after a few minutes because of muscular fatigue and bodily weakness and tumble to the ground, to the great entertainment of the nurses, who would make a circle round him, mocking him with jeers and gibes. The fallen man would have to get up, reascend the stool and take up his position again for the allotted time; if, because of successive falls, he was no longer capable of doing so, the remainder of the punishment would be made up with a certain number of lashes.

The influx of patients was always very great, far in excess of the capacity of the various wards, so to make room for the new arrivals a certain number of patients would be discharged every day, even if not completely recovered and still in a state of serious general debility; despite which they would have to start work again the following day. But those suffering from chronic diseases, or whose stay in hospital had lasted longer than a period of about two months, or who were readmitted too often due to relapses of their illness, were sent – as we have already reported in the case of those with tuberculosis, syphilis or malaria – to Birkenau and there eliminated in the gas chambers. The same fate was suffered by those too depleted to be able to work. Every so often – about once a month – the so-called 'selection of the Muslims'[7] (this picturesque term denoted precisely these extremely emaciated individuals) took place in the various wards of the hospital, with the most physically broken down

7. The use in concentration-camp jargon of the German word *Muselmann* (Muslim) proably derives from the idea, current in Europe in the early twentieth century, that Muslims were believers in Kismet, or destiny. With a black humour that seems shocking to us now (and which reveals something of the brutality of life in the camp) inmates used this term to describe the very different fatalism of prisoners so depleted they had lost the will to survive.

being singled out to be dispatched to the gas chambers. These selections were conducted with great rapidity and were carried out by the doctor in charge of medical services, in front of whom all the patients filed naked, while he judged the general condition of each one with a superficial glance, instantly deciding their fate. A few days later, those selected underwent a second examination by a medical captain in the SS who was the director general of medical services in all the camps subsidiary to Auschwitz. It has to be admitted that this inspection was more thorough than the previous one, with each case being weighed up and discussed; at all events, it was only a lucky few who were removed from the list and readmitted to hospital for further treatment or sent to some Commando where the work was regarded as light; the majority were condemned to death. One of us was included in the list of 'Muslims' no fewer than four times, and escaped each time from a fatal outcome, thanks simply to the fact of being a doctor; since – we do not know whether as a general rule or through an initiative on the part of the administration of the Monowitz Camp – doctors were spared from such a fate.

In October 1944, the selection, instead of being restricted to the wards of the hospital, was extended to all the 'blocks'; but this was the last one, since after that date this kind of exercise was discontinued and the gas chambers at Birkenau were demolished. Nevertheless, 850 victims were selected during that tragic day, among them eight Jews of Italian nationality.

The work of operating the gas chambers and the adjacent crematorium was carried out by a special Commando which worked day and night, in two shifts. The members of this Commando lived in isolation, carefully segregated from any contact with other prisoners or with the outside world. Their clothes gave off a sickening stench, they were always filthy and they had an utterly savage appearance, just like wild animals. They were picked from amongst the worst criminals, convicted of serious and bloody crimes.[8]

It appears that in February 1943 a new crematorium oven and gas chamber were inaugurated at Birkenau, more functional than those which had been in operation up to that month. These consisted of three areas: the waiting room, the 'shower room', and the ovens. At the centre of the ovens rose a tall chimney, around which were nine ovens with four openings each, all of them allowing the passage of three corpses at a time. The capacity of each oven was two thousand corpses a day.

8. See Introduction p. 14 above.

The victims would be ushered into the first room and ordered to undress completely, because – they were told – they had got to take a shower. To make the foul deception more credible, they were handed a piece of soap and a towel, after which they were made to enter the 'shower room'. This was a very large room equipped with fake shower fittings, and with conspicuous signs on the walls saying things like, 'Wash thoroughly, because cleanliness is health', 'Don't economize on soap', 'Remember not to leave your towel here!', so as to make the place look just like a large public bath-house. In the flat ceiling of the room there was a large aperture, hermetically closed by three big metal plates that opened with a valve. A set of rails traversed the whole breadth of the chamber, leading from it to the ovens. When everyone had entered the gas chamber, the doors would be locked (they were airtight) and a chemical preparation in the form of a coarse powder, blue-grey in colour, would be dropped through the valve in the ceiling. It was in metal containers whose labels read: 'Zyklon B – For the destruction of all kinds of vermin', and carried the trade mark of a factory in Hamburg. In fact it was a preparation of cyanide which evaporated at a certain temperature. In the course of a few minutes, all those locked into the gas chamber would die; and then the doors and windows would be flung open, and the members of the Special Commando, equipped with gas masks, would enter in order to take the corpses to the crematorium ovens.

Before putting the bodies into the ovens, a specially designated squad would cut off the hair from those who still had it, that is, from the corpses of those who, as soon as they arrived with their transports, were immediately taken to be slaughtered without entering the camps; and they also extracted the gold teeth from those who had them. The ashes, it is well known, were then scattered in fields and vegetable gardens as a fertilizer for the soil.

Towards the end of 1944, orders reached the Monowitz Camp that all doctors present in the Camp were to be released from working in the Commandos and employed in the various sections of the hospital, as doctors or, in the absence of available posts, as nurses. Before being assigned to their new duties, they had to spend a month gaining experience in the various clinical and surgical departments, following a certain rota, and at the same time they had to take a theoretical training course on the medical organization of the concentration camps and how they were run, the characteristic pathology of the camps and the treatments to be practised on the patients. These orders were duly carried out and the course began in early January 1945; but towards the middle of the same month it was broken off due to the overwhelming Russian offensive in the Kraków-Katowice-Wrocław direction, in the face of which the German forces gave themselves up to headlong flight. The Monowitz Camp was evacuated, along with all the others in the region of Auschwitz, and the Germans dragged about 11,000 prisoners along with them, who, according to information received later from someone who made a miraculous escape, were almost all slaughtered by bursts of machine-gun fire a few days later, when the soldiers escorting them realized that they were completely surrounded by the Red Army and so no longer had any way open to retreat. They had already travelled some seventy kilometres on foot, almost without stopping and with no food, since the provisions they received before leaving the Camp had consisted only of a kilogram of bread, 75 grams of margarine, 90 grams of sausage and 45 of sugar. Later they had been loaded onto various trains which, though taking various different directions, were unable to reach any destination. The massacre then took place of the survivors of such superhuman exertions; many – perhaps three or four thousand – who had stopped on the road, overcome by fatigue, had already been butchered on the spot by pistol shots or by the gun-butts of the soldiers escorting them.

Meanwhile only about a thousand incapacitated, sick or convalescent prisoners who were unable to walk had been left in the Camp, under the surveillance of a few SS men who had been ordered to shoot them before leaving. We do not know why this final order was not carried out, but whatever the reason may have been, it is to this alone that the present writers owe the fact that they are still alive. They had been kept back in the hospital, one detailed to give medical aid to the patients and the other because he was convalescent. The order to take care of the patients could not be carried out except in terms of moral support, since material aid was rendered impossible by the fact that, before abandoning the Camp, the Germans had the hospital stripped of every drug and every surgical instrument; there was no longer so much as an aspirin tablet, a pair of forceps or a gauze dressing.

There followed some highly dramatic days; many patients died from lack of treatment, and many from depletion, since there was also a lack of food. The water mains had been destroyed in an air raid which took place just at this time, so there was no water either. Only the chance discovery of a cache of potatoes, buried in a nearby field to protect them from frost, enabled the least enfeebled to feed themselves and to hold out until the day the Russians finally arrived and made generous provision for the distribution of food.

Glossary of Medical and Pharmaceutical Terms

Proprietary names of drugs are those in use during the 1940s.

Albumin tannate: a compound of tannin with albumin, used in the treatment of diarrhoea.

Alimentary dystrophy: wasting caused by malnutrition.

Anorexia: the prisoners' loss of appetite was not, of course, the psychological illness anorexia nervosa, but was due to their physical condition.

Antipyretic: fever-reducing.

Atropine: a drug derived from belladonna (deadly nightshade); used as a muscle relaxant, as a treatment for biliary colic (severe abdominal pain due to gallstones), and also before anaesthesia to decrease bronchial, salivary and intestinal secretions.

Autohemotherapy: repeated subcutaneous or intramuscular injections of the patient's own blood; formerly practised as a treatment for conditions including skin disorders, syphilis and blackwater fever.

Belladonna: see atropine.

Caffeine: used medicinally as a stimulant for the heart and the central nervous system, and as a mild diuretic.

Calcium: needed by the body for neuromuscular activity and blood-clotting, as well as to maintain the strength of bones and teeth. Calcium gluconate can be used intravenously to treat cases of severe calcium deficiency, which would have been likely to occur in the Monowitz Camp, since the prisoners' diet was almost completely deficient in dairy foods.

Camphorated oil: cottonseed oil infused with camphor; used externally as a counter-irritant.

Cardiazol: proprietary name for a preparation of pentamethylenetetrazol; used in the treatment of respiratory tract and cardiovascular disorders.

Charcoal: medicinal charcoal can be used for its adsorptive properties in the treatment of diarrhoea and as an antidote to various poisons.

Chinosol: a proprietary name for oxyquinolone sulphate; used as an antiseptic.

Collargol: a colloidal preparation of silver, used as an antiseptic.

Coramine: used as a coronary vasodilator (an agent to increase blood flow through the heart) and as a respiratory stimulant.

Desquamation: flaking or peeling of the outer layer of the skin.

Dystrophic diseases: wasting diseases.

Empyema: the accumulation of pus in the pleural cavity (the potential space between the membranes covering the surface of the lung).

Epithelialization: the regrowth of epithelium (the protective surface layer of cells covering the cutaneous layer) over the raw area of a wound in the final stage in the healing process.

Epsom salts: magnesium sulphate, a purgative used for rapid bowel evacuation.

Erysipelas: an acute streptococcal infection causing inflammation of the skin, especially of the face; sometimes called Saint Anthony's fire because of the red, painful rash which characterizes it.

Ethyl chloride: used as a local anaesthetic for minor surgery because of the intense cold produced as it evaporates, and also as a general anaesthetic for short operations.

Evipal: soluble evipal (the sodium salt of evipal) was used intravenously as an anaesthetic for short operations.

Exanthemata: diseases (such as measles and chickenpox) characterized by a rash or the skin signs accompanying a fever.

Fever therapy: Following the discovery by the Austrian neuropsychiatrist Julius von Wagner-Jauregg, in 1877, that tertiary syphilis patients inoculated with malaria would go into remission, the inducing of artificial fever through the use of vaccines and other methods was practised for syphilis and various other diseases until the introduction of the sulphonamide drugs.

Granulomas: small, fleshy masses (granulation tissue) formed in wounds as a response to infection or inflammation.

Hexamethylenetetramine: used in the treatment of chronic or recurrent lower urinary tract infections.

Hydrochloric acid: dilute hydrochloric acid can be used in the treatment of gastrointestinal disorders.

Ichthyol: proprietary name for sulphonated bitumen, a thick, brownish, strong-smelling liquid derived from the distillation of a bituminous schist containing the remains of fish and other marine creatures; used in skin diseases.

Impetigo: a contagious, inflammatory skin disease, usually affecting the face, characterized by pustules which rupture and become crusted.

Lysol: proprietary name for a disinfectant made from a solution of coal tar oil in soap.

Metastatic infiltration: the development of secondary foci of a disease or infection at a distance from the primary site. (Metastasis is the transfer of disease from one organ or part of the body to another not directly connected with it.)

Mitigal: proprietary name for a sulphur-based preparation used to treat scabies.

Oedema: hunger oedema (also known as famine, prison or war oedema) is a form of dropsy, caused by malnutrition, in which fluid seeps from blood vessels and accumulates under the skin, causing local or general swelling.

Ophthalmology: the treatment of eye conditions.

Otitis: inflammation of the ear.

Otorhinolaryngologist: ear, nose and throat specialist.

Panflavin: proprietary name for lozenges containing acri-
flavium chloride, a slow-acting disinfectant; used for
infections of the mouth and throat. In effect, the
diphtheria sufferers at Monowitz who were given Panflavin were being treated for a killer disease with throat
pastilles. Panflavin was manufactured by Bayer, part of
the IG Farben conglomerate.

Pellidol: an antiseptic used topically to promote wound
healing.

Pepsin: general name for the enzymes in the gastric juice.
Pepsin derived from pigs' stomachs was used in mixtures
for dyspepsia for its supposed benefit in aiding digestion.

Petechial: characterized by small red or purple spots
caused by bleeding into the skin.

Phial: small glass bottle for storing drugs to be administered by injection.

Phlegmon: inflammation of the subcutaneous connective
tissue, leading to ulceration and the formation of
invasive abscesses.

Polyneuritis: inflammation of the peripheral nerves which
can be caused by vitamin deficiency, especially of
thiamine (Vitamin B_1).

Pre-agonal: preceding the moment of death.

Pro die: daily.

Prontosil: the first of the sulphonamide drugs; originally developed as a colour-fast red dye, its medicinal properties were discovered by Gerhard Domagk in 1935. It was manufactured by Bayer, part of the IG Farben conglomerate. Germany's superiority in the production of synthetic dyes, on which the Farben empire was based, led to equal success in the pharmaceutical industry.

Purgatin: a laxative used to treat constipation and also for bowel evacuation prior to surgery.

Pyloroplasty: widening of the pylorus, the opening between the stomach and the duodenum (the upper portion of the small intestine) to improve drainage from the stomach.

Pyramidon: a proprietary brand of aminopyrine, an antipyretic and analgesic (used in pain relief).

Rib resection: surgical removal of a portion of rib.

Salts of bismuth: bismuth subnitrate and other bismuth salts can be used in the treatment of gastrointestinal disorders, diarrhoea and dyspepsia.

Scabies: an extremely contagious skin disease, character-ized by severe itching and a red, blister-like rash; caused by Sarcoptes scabiei, the itch-mite.

Seropurulent suppuration: the discharge of a mixture of serum and pus.

Silver nitrate: this was applied externally, either in dilute or pencil form, for its caustic effect.

Sodium bicarbonate: used in medicine as a gastric antacid; also used in solution as an enema and as a dressing for wounds.

Strychnine: formerly used as a central nervous system stimulant. Since it is extremely poisonous, it can be used as a means of suicide, which may be one reason for its absence from the Monowitz pharmacopoeia.

Sulphonamides: a group of drugs derived from sulphani-lamide (originally developed as a colour-fast red dye) which transformed the treatment of diseases such as puerperal fever, meningitis, erysipelas and gonorrhea by preventing the multiplication of bacteria, thus allowing the body's own defence system to fight off the infection.

Sycosis: severe inflammation of the hair follicles, caused by bacterial infection.

Tineas: the various types of ringworm, caused by fungal infections of the skin.

Zinc oxide: a mild astringent (an agent which contracts organic tissue, thus reducing secretion or bleeding); used in various skin conditions.

Bibliography

In compiling this glossary, I have made use of the following:

Blackwell's Nursing Dictionary, Dawn Freshwater and Sian E. Maslin (eds). Oxford: Blackwell Publishing, 2005.

Butterworths Medical Dictionary, Macdonald Critchley (ed.) London, Boston etc.: Butterworths, 1978.

Churchill Livingstone's Dictionary of Nursing, 18th edition, Chris Brooker (ed.) Edinburgh, London, New York etc.: Churchill Livingstone, 2002.

Cornwell, John, *Hitler's Scientists: Science, War and the Devil's Pact*. London: Penguin, 2003.

Dorland, W.A. Newland, *The American Illustrated Medical Dictionary*. Philadelphia and London: W.B. Saunders Co., 1948.

Duncan, T., and Stout, M., *War Surgery and Medicine*. Christchurch, New Zealand: Official History of New Zealand in the Second World War 1939–45, 1954.

Garfield, Simon, *Mauve: How One Man Invented a Colour that Changed the World*. London: Faber and Faber, 2000.

Hayes, Peter, *Industry and Ideology: IG Farben in the Nazi Era*. Cambridge: CUP, 1987.

Martindale: The Extra Pharmacopoeia, 29th edition, James E.F. Reynolds (ed.) and 34th edition, Sean C. Sweetman (ed.) London and Chicago: The Pharmaceutical Press, 2005.

McGrew, Roderick E., *Encyclopedia of Medical History*. London: Macmillan, 1985.

McNair Wilson, R., *British Medicine*. London: William Collins, 1941.

Ogg, Barb and Cochran, Soni, *Mites Medically Important to Humans*.
http://lancaster.unl.edu/enviro/pest/275-97.htm

Oxford Dictionary of Nursing, 4th edition, Elizabeth A. Martin (ed.) Oxford: OUP, 2003.

Sebastian, Anton, *A Dictionary of the History of Medicine*. New York and London: The Parthenon Publishing Group, 1999.

The British Pharmaceutical Codex, 1923: An Imperial Dispensatory for the Use of Medical Practitioners and Pharmacists. London: The Pharmaceutical Press, 1923.

In *Memory of a Good Man (1983)*
Primo Levi

I should like to contribute to the commemoration of
a man who has been close to me for many years,
who shared my harshest experiences, who gave help
to many and asked for help from few, who once
saved my life, and who died quietly a few days ago at
the age of eighty-five. He was a doctor; I think he
must have had thousands of patients during his half
century of professional practice, all of whom have
retained a grateful and affectionate memory of him,
as you do of someone who has assisted you to the
best of his ability, without arrogance and without
intrusion, but entering fully into your problems (and
not only your health problems) in order to help you
overcome them.

He was not good-looking; he was delightfully ugly, something of which he was cheerfully aware and which he exploited as a comic actor might exploit a mask. He had a big, crooked nose and thick, bushy, blond eyebrows which framed a pair of shining blue eyes, never melancholy, almost child-like. In recent years he became deaf, which did not distress him in the least, but even before that he had a way all of his own of taking part in a conversation. If it interested him, he would participate with courtesy and common sense, without ever raising his voice (which in any case was weak and tremulous even when he was a young man); if it did not interest him, or ceased to interest him, he would let his thoughts visibly wander, without doing anything to hide it; he would withdraw into his shell like a tortoise, leaf through a book, look at the ceiling or stroll around the room as if he was on his own.

But he was never absent-minded, indeed he was very attentive, when he was with his patients. By contrast, his feats of absent-mindedness when on holiday were legendary, and he would recount them afterwards with pride; indeed, he often boasted about his weaknesses, which were few, and never about his virtues, which were patience, affection and a quiet courage. Apparently frail, he possessed a rare strength of mind which showed itself more in endurance than in action and which communicated itself invaluably to those who were close to him.

I do not know much about his life before 1943; from then onwards it was not a fortunate one. He was Jewish, and to avoid being captured by the Germans he attempted, in the autumn of that year, to cross the border into Switzerland along with a large group of relatives. They all managed to pass the frontier, but the Swiss guards were unyielding, admitting only the elderly and the children along with their parents. All the others were escorted back to the Italian border: in other words, into the hands of the Fascists and the Germans. We met in the Italian transit camp at Fossoli and were deported together, and from then on we did not part from each other again until our return to Italy in October 1945.

On entering the Lager, his wife, who was as gentle, defenceless and quick to defend others as him, was immediately put to death. He declared that he was a doctor, but he did not know German, so he shared the common fate: labouring in the mud and the snow, pushing wagons, shovelling coal, earth and gravel. It was punishingly hard work for everyone but lethal for him, physically weak, out of condition and no longer young. After a few days on the construction site his shoes injured his feet, which swelled up, and he had to be admitted to the infirmary.

Here there were frequent inspections by the SS doctors; they judged him to be incapable of working and put him on the list for death by gas, but fortunately his professional colleagues, the French or Polish prisoner-doctors of the infirmary, intervened: four times they managed to have his name crossed off. But in the intervals between these death sentences and temporary reprieves he remained as he was, frail but not broken by the brutal life of the Lager, mildly and calmly aware, a friend to everyone, incapable of rancour, without anguish and without fear.

We were liberated together; together we travelled thousands of kilometres in distant lands, and on that interminable and inexplicable journey too his kindly and indomitable character, his infectious capacity for hope and his zeal as a medical practitioner with no medicines were invaluable not only to us, the very few survivors of Auschwitz, but to a thousand other Italian men and women on the uncertain journey back from exile.

Having finally returned to Turin, he stood out

from all the other survivors by his perseverance in keeping alive the network of solidarity among his fellow prisoners, even those far off or in foreign countries. From then on, he lived for almost forty years in a situation that only a man like him would have been able to create around himself: single in registry office terms but in reality surrounded by a multitude of friends, old and new, all of whom felt indebted to him for something: many for their health, others for a wise piece of advice, others still simply for his presence and for his smile, childlike but never unmindful or sad, which lightened the heart.

Leonardo de Benedetti (1983)
Primo Levi

On 16 October this year, Dr Leonardo De Benedetti died suddenly in the Jewish Rest Home where he had lived for several years. He was eighty-five years old; formerly the municipal doctor of Rivoli,[1] he was arrested in 1943 while trying to leave the country and deported to Auschwitz, where he lost his wife. In the Lager, his status as a doctor was not recognized; he spent almost a year there, enduring hunger, cold, fatigue and alienation with a rare serenity and strength of mind which communicated itself to anyone who had occasion to speak with him. Liberated in January 1945 by the Soviet army, he had the task of organizing an infirmary in the transit

1. A small town outside Turin

camp at Katowice; resources were few but his zeal was great, and news of the Italian doctor who listened to everyone and treated everyone gratis spread out in a wide circle, so that not only Italian ex-prisoners but also foreign ones came to him, as did many Polish townsfolk and even some Soviet soldiers.

After a long and adventurous journey of repatriation, he settled in Turin and resumed the practice of his profession. His patience, experience and humanity were such that all his patients soon became his friends and turned to him for advice and help. He did not enjoy solitude, and at first he lived with relatives and then with a family of friends: Dr Arrigo Vita and his two sisters. They passed away one after another and Dr De Benedetti was left on his own. Until he was eighty, the age at which he retired from his profession, he had been the hard-working and highly esteemed doctor of the Rest Home, where he decided to take up residence in the serene sadness of one who knows he has not lived in vain; but he was never alone there: every day until his last he would receive visits and invitations from loving relatives, from friends and colleagues and from fellow prisoners. He also used to receive a great many letters, even from foreign countries, because no one who had met him ever forgot him, and he would reply to all of them, even the tiresome ones, with punctilious care.

Last spring he experienced the first symptoms of the disease to which he would eventually succumb; he gave himself the sensible medical treatment which his long experience suggested and continued to live in peace of mind, taking no risks and feeling no fear. Death took him suddenly and mercifully without making him suffer. He was a brave and gentle man who had been an invaluable help to many while never asking for help from anyone.